Plants in My World

WHAT ARE SEEDS?

Jens Haakonsen

HABA®

PowerKiDS press.

NEW YORK

Published in 2018 by The Rosen Publishing Group, Inc.
29 East 21st Street, New York, NY 10010

First Edition

Editor: Theresa Morlock
Book Design: Michael Flynn

Photo Credits: Cover, p. 21 Ekaterina Kondratova/Shutterstock.com; p. 5 Marie C Fields/Shutterstock.com; p. 6 amenic181/Shutterstock.com; p. 9 Chad Springer/Getty Images; p. 10 kram9/Shutterstock.com; p. 13 Jason Loucas/Getty Images; p. 14 Aleksei Stebiuk/Shutterstock.com; p. 17 Romolo Tavani/Shutterstock.com; p. 18 Teri Virbickis/Shutterstock/com; p. 22 Alistair Berg/Getty Images.

Cataloging-in-Publication Data

Names: Haakonsen, Jens.
Title: What are seeds? / Jens Haakonsen.
Description: New York : PowerKids Press, 2018. | Series: Plants in my world | Includes index.
Identifiers: ISBN 9781508161554 (pbk.) | ISBN 9781508161578 (library bound) | ISBN 9781508161561 (6 pack)
Subjects: LCSH: Seeds–Juvenile literature.
Classification: LCC QK661.H33 2018 | DDC 581.4'67–dc23

Manufactured in China

CPSIA Compliance Information: Batch #BS17PK: For Further Information contact Rosen Publishing, New York, New York at 1-800-237-9932

Please visit: www.rosenpublishing.com and www.habausa.com

CONTENTS

What's a Seed?

A seed is where a plant comes from!
Seeds come in all shapes and sizes. They
can be small or big. They can be round or
pointy. Seeds come in all different colors.

Growing Seeds

To grow into a plant, a seed must be buried in the soil. In the soil, seeds start to change. Roots spread into the soil. A stem grows above the soil.

Plants need sunlight and water. They also need air. Plants turn sunlight, water, and air into the energy they need to grow. This is called photosynthesis.

A young plant is called a seedling. A young tree is called a sapling. Some plants die within a season. Trees can live for hundreds of years.

Saplings need to grow into trees before they can grow fruit. Oranges, apples, and cherries are common fruit trees in America.

14

Inside a Fruit

Inside every fruit is a seed or a pit that can be planted to grow a new tree. Fruit that falls from branches can be carried away by animals that eat them.

Seeds can also be spread by the wind.
When a dandelion is ready to spread its
seeds, it turns white and fluffy. The seeds are
carried away on the wind.

17

All Kinds of Seeds

Fruits with pits are called stone fruits. Cherries, peaches, and avocados are stone fruits.

It's important to take the pit out of your fruit when you eat it.

Some kinds of seeds can make people sick. Eating too many apple seeds can be bad for you. Other kinds of seeds, like watermelon seeds, are safe to eat.

Some seeds grow into plants, trees, and flowers. They're spread by the wind or by animals that eat them. You can plant seeds to grow your very own garden!

WORDS TO KNOW

dandelion

seedling

soil

INDEX